BEYOND A COTTAGE WINDOW

Beyond a Cottage Window

MARY ROBERTS

Illustrated by
MICHAEL CHARLTON

TO MY HUSBAND PETER
~ right up to the moon and back

I will make you brooches and toys for your delight
Of bird-song at morning and star-shine at night.
I will make a palace fit for you and me,
Of green days in forests and blue days at sea.

Robert Louis Stevenson

First published in the United Kingdom in 2003 by
The Hobnob Press, PO Box 1838, East Knoyle, Salisbury SP3 6FA

British Library Cataloguing in Publication Data: A catalogue record for this book is available from the British Library.
ISBN 0-946418-18-7
Typeset in 12/16pt Scala. Typesetting and origination by John Chandler
Printed in Great Britain by Salisbury Printing Company Ltd, Salisbury

CONTENTS

PREFACE

Over thirty years ago my husband Peter and I came from Bedfordshire to Pond Cottage in the Wiltshire Downs, Peter for the garden at the Manor House and me to look after ponies, dogs, chickens and other small animals.

This book tells of life in the countryside as seen by a gardener's wife and cottager (the dictionary lists cottager as 'one who dwells in a cottage, especially of labourers'). So be it!

The countryside surrounding the cottage is rolling downland where once lived prehistoric man, who left us many barrows and tumuli, Stonehenge and Avebury's stone circles. Then came the Romans, with their camps and roads, later the Saxons, and here King Alfred fought many battles against the invading Danes. That ancient past can still be felt on the hill tops, where Skylarks sing and the call of the Plover can be heard.

Here, on the short soft springy turf, many of the country's greatest racehorses have been trained, their

galloping hooves flying over the wild flowers that thrive on chalk land, among them the wild Thyme which, in summer, provides nectar for bees and butterflies of all description, whilst in winter the Downs have their own lovely wild loneliness.

Included in this book are many old country sayings, gardening and farming lore, from all parts of the country which I have gathered together, watching through the cottage window as seasons come and go.

I wish to give my thanks to Peter my husband for his encouragement at all times; to my dear friend Eileen Jenkins for her hard work in helping to make my writing readable; to Michael Charlton for his delightful illustrations; and to John Chandler of Hobnob Press for publishing this book. . . . Also to Pond Cottage where I find the peace and background for my writing.

Mary Roberts
31 July 2003

I POND COTTAGE

STONES OF GOLD

The cottages stand on their ancient stones
And gaze at the modern scene.
As if to say 'We've seen it all,
And all that is good has been'.
But once they too were brash and new,
And a change from the Tudor style.
Times move on and change will come
As the hands move round the dial.
But those that love the solid and old
Will cherish and value strong stones of gold.

Barbara Kimber

THE COTTAGE, probably 300 years old, is built of Sarsen stone, and once was thatched. It was altered many years ago with the upper storey of red fish-tail tiles and slate roof. Through its many years it has settled into the surrounding countryside, as if it had grown there. In the spring the nooks and crannies of its joists and joints, stones and tiles, become the home of many birds – Sparrows, Bluetits, Starlings (a pair come back each year to build behind the loose tile near to our bedroom window, and I swear they wear hobnailed boots, because they make such a noise). They vie amongst themselves for the choicest nesting sites. Such chirping, singing and bird arguments go on from dawn to dusk, while the ridge tiles on the roof give the best lookout for the cock Blackbird, whose nest is close by in the old lilac bush. He sings his praises whilst his bright eyes miss nothing, and his wife, sitting snuggly on her nest of mud lined with grass, containing a clutch of five eggs, is lulled by his singing and the sweet waft of perfume from her lilac bower.

The old sarsen stones, warmed by the summer sun, take on a glow of colour, deep lilac pink and grey, whilst the newly added bathroom and kitchen of brash red brick is now covered with ivy, making warm resting places during the winter months for many small creatures.

The cottage is not just a home for we humans. Many other small creatures share our shelter. A swarm of bees lives for part of the summer in a hole at the bottom of a door jamb, where a piece of wood has rotted away. A few beetles wander across the floor at times and, alas, mice do venture in. They are not encouraged to stay. Spiders are asked politely to leave, but rarely do: and the Ladybirds seem to find us mildly interesting. Dogs and cats have lived happily here with us, sharing our hearth, home and board. Benjamin the donkey, as a baby, came into the house with us, but that is another story. The cottage has given shelter to many during its time, and these people seem to have left a sense of peace within its thick walls.

The old fireplace, built of sarsen stone, has been opened up and a good log fire burns on its hearth during the winter. Along its beam and down the sides of the fireplace hang the horse brasses brought with us long ago from the old farmhouse at Priestley in Bedfordshire. On the hearth stand the copper kettles and brass trivets, all homely and loved things. In early summer the brass preserving pan hangs there full of Cow Parsley and, from the open doorway, the scent of Wallflowers, Lily of the Valley and Sweet-brier wafts into the room amidst the sound of birds and humming bees.

By the fireside stand the two old leather armchairs, which belonged to my husband's family. 'Why don't you get rid of those shabby worn old armchairs?' is so often said to me. I look at them, so very worn about the arms and seat springs sagging – but the backs! Still the hide shines like polished chestnuts and the lovely wood carvings on the front of the arms still gleam. 'All they need is a good polish and new cushions, ' I'd say. 'She's mad!' I hear them think. But I know things they would never dream of when sitting in their very modern centrally heated rooms.

I look at the chairs, and a head peeps over the arm, with spotted nose and long silky ears. She rests her head where so many faithful heads have rested over the years, and her eyes say 'I'm so happy, warm and safe here'. (Of course, we turn the cushions over when there are guests in best attire, and she sits disconsolately on the rug!).

The arms were worn with hands that, restless with illness, fretted at the inactivity, but I see Father's grey head against the polished back, and hear again the many stories oft told . . . 'of the magnificent sow, eight black, eight white she had. And how Lizzy Condor, an upstanding woman, always had her cake cut thick, and many, many more tales of animals'-farm language. Many hours he waited for his sons' return from war, and here he met their future wives and heard their plans for future days.

The chairs are still here with us. So many happy days they have seen. They have held us in our joys and in our sorrows, and helped us with the children's play – 'Grandmother's shopping basket' – and many more games. They have been jumped up and down on with joy, and held us when we wept for those we loved, now gone, and in the firelight's reflection you can curl up, dream and be warm and comforted. Still they smell of wood smoke and good leather polish (a little, perhaps, at times, of wet dog, but then, who cares?) I swear I catch them wink when someone says 'why don't you get rid of those old chairs?'

IVY LEAVES

GLOSSY GREEN ivy leaves, dark stained traced with light green veins, just the backgrounds for a bunch of snowdrops, tied with wool, gathered beneath the hedge and from round the bole of the Beech tree, where they grow in drifts. Just a few taken from each clump, their delicate faintly green-edged petals supported by cool slender stalks. A miracle in the cold rough winds how such fragile beauty survives to shake its head in the wind and bring hope and brightness into our lives. How joyfully we greet the first snowdrops in the dark dreary days, and then to search among the mosses on the sunny bank for the first Violets, until one still sunny morning, passing the bank where only a few days past we found the first buds. We are assailed with a waft of surely the most wonderful of scents, that of the wild white Violets in full bloom.

Higher on the bank is a clump of Celandine, pure gold, with the leaves so specially glossed dark green to enrich the golden crown. A Chaffinch sings on a bough above – wait patiently and quietly and watch and no doubt you will find he has a nest somewhere in the hedge in the fork of the old thorn tree growing nearby. A nest made of mosses, lichens and pieces of soft wool, lined with feathers, hair and soft down. The hair from my Springer Spaniel's coat is a great favourite with birds for the lining of their nests, it is so soft and silky.

The old tree, from which we took the ivy leaves for the snowdrops, has a thick trunk covered with ivy. Many times I have thought to pull away the ivy to spare the tree. Though I do wonder if ivy does damage the tree as much as is supposed? Then I think of all the small wildlife that uses the ivy for its shelter and for food. Many a nest is there in Summer, and during Winters cold and stormy nights what shelter is provides! The old tree seems strong and healthy. From its topmost branches a pair of pigeons survey their poor attempts at a nest below. A Tree Creeper scampers mouse-like along a branch, its silvery breast just catching the sun. The Great Spotted Woodpecker peers nervously round a branch, his red nape catching our eye. He peeps to see if his favourite pudding or bone is on the bird table.

Early in the morning a Thrush sings its morning psalm to its God. From the topmost branch the sun's rays lighting the spotted downy breast and, looking up, I am reminded of Hopkins's poem 'Pied Beauty', 'Glory be to God for dappled things'.

The old Spaniel is at my feet, her paws and breast are as dappled as the Thrush and, though her song is not as sweet as his, her devotion to her God is as pure.

Whose song is the sweetest? the Thrush
Or the Blackbird with his flute of wood,
Or the Nightingale whose sweet notes thrill the night time hours,
The little Wren and Robin sing with all their hearts and how often has the Chaffinch lifted our hearts on cold grey March days with its chip, chip cherie?

A poor world it would be for us all without the birdsongs and the flowers, the trees and the beasts of the fields.

2 SPRING

MARCH

THE MONTH OF MARCH is the beginning of a gardener's year. A month so varied in weather with March winds that can be so bitter, making the soil cold but friable. 'A peck of dust in March is worth a King's ransom', is the old saying, and at last when the weather is open, fine and fair, work can begin on the ground.

The kitchen garden to the Manor House is surrounded by an old brick wall which gives shelter from the cold winds. Here the onion sets are planted in long straight rows, set just below the soil to stop those mischievous Blackbirds from pulling them out, no doubt for the grubs that lie beneath them, as the sets themselves are not touched.

The shallots have already been planted, but not always as the 'old'uns' say, 'Plant on the shortest day, pull on the longest.'

A special plot is made ready for growing exhibition onions. The soil double dug and a barrow or two of rich rotted farmyard muck, with a generous helping of wood ash saved from the big open fire in the cottage.

A dry spring can bring its own problems. Badgers, searching for worms or grubs, dig up the lawns which have been watered, especially under an old Cedar tree, which was ailing. It had been treated by the Tree Surgeons, and then had Bullocks Blood fed into it in an effort to save its life. A hose pipe was left running many hours to wash the goodness into its roots. Then, in the night, the Badgers came and what a digging and mess they made. Alas by July 1997 the Cedar tree had died, and a Timber Firm came in and felled it. The old tree which had taken around 200 years to grow had come to its end. A sad day for us who had known it for over thirty years. No longer will the Gold Crests return in the Spring to build their nests in its branches. As I write the room is filled with the scent of Cedar wood. When I said goodbye to the tree, before the trunk was carted away on the timber wagon, I picked up a chunk which had been split away by the woodman's axe, and it is here with me bringing back memories of its great branches giving shade in Summer. Often in Winter it would be covered in snow, a picture of a Winter wonderland.

On one of those bright March days when the sun really warms, I took a basket filled with a pot of home made jam, some cakes and fruit, all covered with a napkin and set out with my dog along the little path that leads by the side of the wood and over the Downs through an old swing gate, there I met a friend from the nearby village. I passed her the basket and we sat awhile for a chat. This was just a short break in a busy day using the old fashioned way by taking the well-worn paths used for centuries. Soon part of the path I used is to be closed owing to security measures of a nearby large racing establishment.

As I walked home, I wondered at the passing of so many things in the country that we have taken for granted. Hedges, once the habitat of so many birds and other forms of wildlife, now grubbed out and destroyed. The old stiles to help us over, or through those hedges, whose top rails were worn smooth by many a steadying hand, the bottom steps a resting place for many a weary foot, or heavy basket. These stiles were made of good solid Oak or Elm differing in design from county to county, but what stories they could tell of lovers' meetings, secrets whispered and bargains made. Many a message or basket was left by the stile to be collected later on. Small children loved to clamber through and over the stile, and place their many coloured 'cooty shells' (snails) along the step to play at shops, whilst their mothers, or grandmothers, rested their tired bodies against the rails and enjoyed a gossip. Now, two pieces of wood cross a wire fence, the step so high from the ground it is an effort to climb on to it, and a work of art to retain one's balance when crossing over the wire. There is no comfort, or rest, from them, no pride of workmanship in their construction. They have no right to the honoured name of stile that has served the country folk so well down the years. They are but 'step overs'!

As I walked home I cross the old Green Street, the path that leads up to the Ridgeway and on down into Avebury. I could see, walking along the path in the distance, a small group of hikers, their backs slightly bowed with their rucksacks. So must the Pilgrims have looked as they trod that same path, to some holy shrine? I made my way home with my dog at heel, and as I breasted the rise I could see below smoke rising from the cottage chimney, so I knew gardening for the day was over and the kettle was singing on the hob.

MOTHERING SUNDAY

WET, COLD AND GREY, but the white and purple Violets are out on the bank beneath the hedges, whilst above on a hawthorn bush a Thrush sings his song of adoration.

Mothering Sunday and the Church is full with children and their parents. There is a christening and the christening party fills the back pews, which are near the old font. The baby's parents, so young and proud, the joy of parenthood shining from them. The baby cocooned in a white shawl peeped out and seemed to enjoy his surroundings. He is christened James Arthur by the Vicar, with all the children crowding round to watch as the holy water is poured gently on his forehead and the sign of the Cross made. A candle burns bright to signify our faith. The most lovely thing of all is when the children go to the Altar to collect a bunch of flowers to hand to their Mothers. The father of James carried him up to the Altar to take a small bunch of yellow Daffodils and Primroses, which he placed on the baby's shawl and, walking back, handed baby and flowers to his wife, a simple but loving gesture.

APRIL

MARCH PASSES into April, and in the grassy bank we find the wild sweet Violets, and hedges and ditches are bright yellow with Celandines. The Daffodils seem to dance in the stiff breeze. Lambs totter beside anxious mothers in the Daisy-covered meadows. But April is not always kind, and often a sharp frost or snow showers bring a halt to planting out in the garden. Then we hope for a gentle April shower to put us all in a good humour again. Each day we look out for a sight of the first Swallow, and the Cuckoo's call. Here, both the Cuckoo and the Swallow seem to arrive about 20 April, and over the wood floats the Cuckoo's call. On the hill the winter sown corn grows taller. We pull, and freeze, the tender forced Rhubarb, such a delicate pink and quite a different flavour to the summer Rhubarb.

The Asparagus is coming through and is watered and weeded, and later in the month the first bunch is cut. Short, fat white stalks and tender purple mouth-watering tips, are neatly tied and placed in the trug basket with some creamy-curded Broccoli, and taken into the back kitchen of the Big House.

The last of the carrots, stored in an old copper for the winter in the potting shed, are cleared out.

The lawn gets its first cut, and the scent of grass mowings mingles with the sweet-briar growing on the wall. Bluebells and Primroses, and the Blackthorn in flower edges the lanes. When Easter falls in April, and the weather is kind, I believe it is the most beautiful time of the year.

On Good Friday we eat hot cross buns, made in our little village, warm and spicy. and delivered to us in a basket covered with a linen napkin fixed with a bunch of Primroses. When we were children, the shepherd who lived in a neighbouring village, walked across the fields with them, and we ate them before our breakfast.

We spend the day quietly. Sometimes the seed (early) Potatoes are planted. Later in the afternoon we walk to the woods, where once we would have picked a few Good Friday Primroses, their cool pink stalks and soft yellow petals bring back memories of other Good Fridays when country folk were allowed to gather Primroses from the Manor woods, and the families met and took tea together to exchange gossip.

On Saturday the Church is decorated for Easter Sunday. The font swathed in Bluebells and Primroses. Daffodils line the windows and pulpit. Pure white Lilies adorn the Altar together with baskets of eggs and the Easter loaf.

The cottage is fresh with polish, and the brass gleams, with a yellow candle in each candlestick. Flowers fill the rooms with sweetness. Easter cards line the shelves, and in the evening, as it grows cold, logs glow on the hearth.

Easter Sunday morning we rise early, for the sun is said to dance as it rises on this Holy day. We take the lane to the little Church and, on entering its doors we are greeted with the scent of all its flowers, mingled with its age-old stone and wood. We sing the familiar hymns and say the old comforting prayers. Then back to the cottage for breakfast. On the sideboard stand the chocolate Easter eggs, not forgetting one for the dog!

Lunch is prepared. The lamb garnished with Rosemary. Vegetables are scrubbed, and soon the aroma of roasting meat fills the cottage, and our appetites are sharpened.

Friends join us in the afternoon, and we walk over the Downs, or sit and chat, according to our age and mobility.

There is a Simnel cake for tea, with its eleven almond paste balls (the eleven paste balls represent the 11 Disciples – alas, the 12th was Judas, who betrayed Christ), and sugar eggs in a green icing nest in the centre.

In the evening we play cards by the fire, and partake of a buffet supper of meat pies, crusty bread, cheese and salads, followed by fruit tart and thick yellow cream, and to drink there is wine, beer or cider. When our friends have departed, we retire to bed, giving thanks for another Easter Sunday.

On Easter Monday a little work is done in the cottage garden. Then we pack a picnic lunch and travel to a Point-to-Point meeting, which is held at a nearby farm.

In the garden everything grows apace. Shrubs are pruned, lawn edges tidied, and sweet pea plants set out in the greenhouse. The tomato plants are potted on from an earlier sowing. Lettuce, cabbage and cauliflower plants are put into the glass frames to harden off ready to plant directly into the vegetable garden at a later date.

Also in April (sometime around 16-21) Swallows and House Martins return to the village after their long flight of many miles across land and sea. Each morning we watch out for them, and with what joy we greet their return. The Cuckoo also arrives around this time. In fact there is an old saying that 'the Cuckoo is let out at Vizes Fair', which takes place around the 19-20 April. Coming through Devizes one 19 April I noticed the Fair on the green by the Crammer, and sure enough the next day I heard my first Cuckoo of the year, and when the Cuckoo is here country folk will say 'Now our troubles will be over'. Alas, I am afraid that is not quite true.

Living in a small village, with no street lights and few dwellings, when the weather is clear, the night sky has many wonders to behold. Stars beyond counting, some easily picked out, like The Plough and The Milky Way, we have known from childhood, and in 1997 the Haley's Comet, with its shimmering tail, was exciting to watch each evening.

The new crescent moon is greeted by bowing, turning over ones money, and making a wish. Everyone knows it is unlucky to see a new moon through glass!

The days lengthen, and before we know it May is here with her lap overflowing with blossom.

MAY

As I sit at an open window on a May morning, with the warm sunshine streaming in, I become aware of a fat bumble bee which has got on the wrong side of the glass, and the bumbling buzz of it makes it hard for me to keep my eyes open, so I give it a little helping hand to show it the way out to where the Wallflowers, Pansies and Tulips await it. Scents from the garden waft up through the open window, filling the room with a mixture of flower scents and freshly mown grass. The blue of the Forget-me-nots mingles with the pink-tipped Daisies, and among them shines the glory of the Dandelion.

The Daffodils are now over, but in the wild garden the Bluebells take their place. The hedges are becoming greener each day, and the Blackthorn that bloomed so profusely through the 'Blackthorn Winter' – Robbie Burns refers to it as 'Milk White is the Slae', certainly lived up to its name. How it conjures up those drifts of snow-white blossoms.

The Chestnut trees have all their candles lit. One of the old country sayings is that each candle of the Chestnut tree shines for a soul that had departed the previous year. As with the Blackthorn there is often a cold snap when the Chestnut is in bloom. Now the sweet blossom of the

Hawthorn (May Blossom), is beginning to show; the tender shoots of the leaves were eaten by the plough boys of long ago and called 'bread and cheese'. The old song 'Here we come gathering nuts in May', I believe should be 'knots of May'. However, I sang as a child 'gathering nuts in May' with the rest of my friends.

Somewhere near sings the Blackbird – its mate safely hidden, brooding her clutch of four or five eggs.

The meadow opposite the cottage is a fresh green and is sparkling with Daisies and newly shorn sheep. Thankfully they are once more united with their lambs. For a while all was bedlam as sheep and lambs were separated for the shearing. Now the lambs have got over the shock of a slim white wool-less mother and have started their lamb games once again.

Why is it in a group of happy gambolling lambs, playing 'King of the Castle', there is always one little knock-kneed fellow, his black woolly socks seeming to be too big for him, standing forlornly watching, as if he is not wanted in their game. Or, has his Mamma warned him of the other lambs' rough behaviour and to keep away?

In the garden the potato shoots are through the ground, and quite often frosts are forecast, so sacks, paper bags and sheets of plastic are found to cover over the tender shoots. Some of the Lilies, which have been planted in the terracotta pots, are covered over with black plastic bags meant for the dustbin. In the early morning, forgetting we have covered over the pots, we turn the corner by the greenhouse and come face to face with a grotesque black object, which almost causes us to have a heart attack, until we realise it is the black-bag-clad Lilies.

As dusk falls the scent of Bluebells from the wood seems to become more pungent. I stand quietly by the old church with the froth of white cherry blossom, like a frilled petticoat against the old grey stones, and I watch a family of rabbits chase round a clump of nettles, amidst the daisies which have suddenly closed their petals. After all, their name implies 'Days eyes'.

I become aware of a barn owl floating by on its silent feathered wings, which brings to mind the old name of the time of day 'owl light'. An apt description for those lovely moments between dusk and darkness. From the Lilac bush a Blackbird still sings, and I know of a wood in Sussex where the Bluebells carpet the ground with a never ending sea of blue. There in the thick hedge surrounding the woods Nightingales will be singing. We used to visit Sussex in May, staying with friends and sitting late into the night listening to those brown birds singing. Happy memories of a dear friend no longer with us.

THE GIFT

AT THE CORNER of the old grey stone cottage, when the field hedges were thick with May blossom and the Bluebells carpeted the Beechwoods, a little brown hen Pheasant brooded nineteen eggs. Her nest was close to the wall under the sweet-brier and hidden from view, by yellow Deadnettles, blue Forget-me-nots and purple Thyme.

We watched each evening as she made her way for a drink and dust bath, often slipping by our old black Labrador sleeping on the lawn. We rerouted visitors by another path so she should not be disturbed. At night the Bats flew above her and from farm buildings came the hoot of the Tawny Owl. Further over in the meadow, a Barn Owl hawked for mice or shrews, but the Pheasant remained safe in her hidden nest – or so we believed! The night the Pheasant chicks hatched I was awakened at first light by a loud hissing noise. Rushing to the window, I saw a large cat gazing into the nest. I shouted and frightened it away, but alas, the damage was done. Scattered round the garden were several dead chicks, so the cat, or something must have come earlier unheard by us. The poor mother Pheasant spent all day in a flower border near the nest. Finally disappearing into the fields in the evening.

Next day, in the flower border from where the hen Pheasant had watched over her ravaged nest, a border which had been dug over each Spring for many years, I found, lying on the surface, a small slim, beautiful blue bottle. I like to think it was a gift from the Pheasant for her cosy nest so near to us. But I am sad when I look at the bottle on the sill of the little window, which overlooks the cottage garden. As the sun lights up the beautiful blue colour, I feel I let her down, that little mother Pheasant. If only I had woken earlier that bright May morning.

LATE SPRING, EARLY JUNE

THE GARDEN and countryside are filled with the song of birds, all our summer visitors are once again back with us after their long arduous flight over many miles of land and sea. The spotted Flycatchers are some of the last to arrive and build their nests in the old red-brick wall surrounding the garden. A brick has broken and become dislodged, and here each year they build their nests of lichen and moss which they have carried from the lawns, and she lays her batch of off-white brownish spotted eggs.

In the meadows the grasses ripen and Buttercups and Milkmaids bloom in profusion. We hold Buttercups beneath our chins to see if we like butter, and Daisy chains are made to decorate young and old alike, and the dog wears a double chain around her neck.

The Quaking (or Totter) grass is a great favourite of mine, growing along the track leading on to the Downs. Each year I find it and take one stem, and however hard I try to hold it still I fail, and with advancing years it has become an impossible task. Now, I take pleasure in just watching the delicate purplish brown spikelets tremble in the lightest of air movements.

The cows browse knee-deep in Buttercups and come more slowly to the cowman's call at milking time.

In the garden Asparagus is cut for the table with a special saw-edged knife. Short thick shoots with purple tips shading down to white when steamed and served with melted butter. It is a dish for the gods.

Strawberries, which have been strawed earlier and netted against thieving Blackbirds, who, having reared their brood with the thought of those bright sweet berries in mind, become very annoyed at being unable to eat their fill (and who can blame them?), are now ready for gathering, and we crawl along the rows filling our baskets, and a few find their way into our mouths. The gathered Strawberries are then covered with a Rhubarb leaf and taken into the kitchen to be eaten for dessert or made into Strawberry jam. One of the best jams to be eaten by the fireside in Winter, with home made scones and cream.

3 SUMMER

A GLIMPSE OF ROCKLEY IN EARLY SUMMER

THE LANE IS SHADED by Elder bushes in full bloom with large plates of tiny creamy blossoms, hanging from the branches, and with the delicate flowers of the Dog Rose entwined among them. There had been a shower of rain earlier, and the sun now drew out the heady perfume of the mingled flowers and grasses, whilst overhead a Blackbird sings from the topmost branch of a May Tree whose blossoms are fast fading.

On the hillside a great splurge of scarlet Poppies spreads among a field of yellow Rape, a colour scheme which should clash, but nature can mix her palette with all the shades and hues she pleases. Suddenly, from a stand of Beech trees, comes the clear call of the Cuckoo, who had been little heard since its arrival in mid-April. W.H. Davies wrote 'a rainbow and a cuckoo's song may never come together again; may never come this side of the tomb'. I understand his feeling. I could come again to this spot a thousand times and not recapture that moment when the sun shone on that brilliant splash of colour and hear at the same time the Cuckoo's call floating above it all. A Cuckoo who had not 'in June changed its tune'.

In the next field Barley shimmers silver in the sun, a light wind ripples wave upon wave of the bearded heads with the effect of a never ending sea washing against a distant shore. Standing there I am mesmerised and have the feeling of drifting far across that rippling sea into a dream world.

> Of days
> When all the world is young, lad.'.
> And all the trees are green
> And every goose a swan, lad
> And every lass a queen
>
> *from the poem 'Young and Old' by Charles Kingsley.*

This lovely Sunday morning I could sit and watch forever the pattern of clouds blown by the strong beeze over the meadow bright with early morning sunshine, and its broad rim of golden nodding Buttercups and patches of deep rosy pink Clovers, while the cattle rest under the Hawthorn tree, which is bright with May blossom.

A family of Rooks is busy about the meadow, the parent bird finding succulent morsels for their hopping swanking children, whose beaks are ever demanding.

A fat Pigeon, whose plumage in the sunlight has a lavender sheen, which complements his white collar, and it looks as if it was specially laundered for Sunday wear.

A cock Pheasant proudly protects his hen Pheasant, who has no doubt just left a nest of eggs to partake of a little refreshment. Her colouring seems drab against the cock's flamboyant purple, green and rust, but her feathers blend into the dead leaves and nettles where she has her nest, keeping her safe from predators' prying eyes and hungry mouths.

From the nearby wood floats the call of the Cuckoo, and over the rolling Downland, carried by the breeze, comes the sound of the nearby village Church bells calling the faithful to prayer.

Walking back from Marlborough along the Downs with our dog, Bonnie, on a sunny though windy morning, with blue skies and Skylarks singing high above the Winter-sown corn, I came across a wreath of flowers, now faded, but which had once been a mass of white Carnations and green foliage. It had been placed by the side of one of the 'Racehorse Gallops' on the spot where an Irishman suffered a heart attack and fell from the horse he was riding. He died there on those gallops, and the last thing he must have seen was that unspoilt loveliness of those rolling Downs, with the song of the Skylark soaring above him. There, on the close cropped turf, someone, with love and sorrow, had placed a wreath of flowers. Those who passed the spot would pause and perhaps whisper a prayer, not only for the one gone from the Downs, but for those who still walk or ride on this cherished Downland.

JULY

ONE JULY MORNING, after a rough windy night, we found, lying beneath the electricity wires where they joined a junction box, a dead Barn Owl. No doubt it had hit the wires whilst out hunting the stockyard nearby for mice. Such a beautiful creature, even in death. The ears hidden under layers of feathers, huge openings compared to the rest of its body. The feathers, shading from rich buff to pure white, so clean and unsullied. The eyes no longer seeing, and the powerful talons relaxed. It was wonderful, though so sad, to see at such close quarters this night-flying bird, whose wing span is so large but whose weight is so little, who, apart from their (some think) eerie call, move so softly and quietly through the night. We were afraid it was the Owl that lived in the end of the old school (long since closed) next to our cottage, and whose nightly sorties along the edge of the Downs we watched from the garden as we drank our last cup of coffee before going to bed, the evening air sweet with the perfume of Roses and Honeysuckle, mingled with the lovely milky smell of cattle grazing in the meadow beyond the lane. Thankfully, the following night, just as we were drifting off to sleep, we heard the call from the top of the telegraph pole, and there sat our Owl. How good it was to know it was still with us. But sad to think perhaps its friend, or mate, had gone. The Barn Owls are fast dwindling, as is so much of our hitherto taken for granted country wild life.

Later on in August that year, whilst pushing a wheel barrow over the lawn, my husband Peter nearly ran over what he at first thought was a Wren, but on closer examination found it to be a young Goldcrest. Both blinked hard at each other, whilst the mother Goldcrest had hysterics in the Cedar tree, above where she had her nest and from which the little one had tumbled. After Peter had admired and blessed the little creature, he left it to its mother to remove it to safer quarters, and he continued on his way to prepare his vegetables and flowers for the annual Flower Show to be held in the village hall the following week.

THE FLOWER SHOW

HANDS SO BROWN, blunt fingers, sure among the rounded potatoes, the long slender beans, the fat comfortable peas, creamy cauliflowers and glowing beet. Knowing which ones to choose to catch the Judge's eye. Fingers so strong, but gentle, not to rub bloom from pod or delicate petal. So firm in tying down the tops of great squat gleaming onions. Firstly placing into vase or pot, the chosen

spray or single Rose or smiling Pansy. Hands that have tended the cherished flower or vegetable from seedtime to harvest. The same hands, well scrubbed with soap and brush, will later take with pride from the gloved hand, the coveted card or cup, to place among the other gleanings of past shows. The memories of which enliven many a firelit Winter evening when hands are idle, except to turn and mark the seed catalogue for the coming season. To choose and ponder on perhaps another fancy which should do well for the Village Show come next year.

9 AUGUST 1993

TODAY, AN OLD well-loved inhabitant of the village was laid to rest in the town cemetery. He rests there with his wife. His daughter, who died when a baby, is buried in the little graveyard in the village. His funeral service was a short one, with two hymns, 'Abide with Me , and 'The day thou, gavest Lord is ended'. He lived, as a small boy, at a nearby farm, and went to school in the village and sang in the Church Choir. One of his first jobs was as 'Boot Boy' at the nearby farm. He then stayed on to work for the farmer. He moved to a cottage in the village and lived there until his boss, the farmer, retired. He then moved into the town. He was a true country-man, and we will miss his stories of his work carried out in the fields and with animals. He was shepherd as well as cowman, and now in the village, as night draws near, one can imagine the sound of the bells coming from the sheep once folded on the Downs and his words 'they latten bells do sound best of all'. Just now loads of straw from the freshly harvested fields go by. He saw and helped with so many harvests from those same fields. Perhaps we should have added one more hymn at his funeral, 'All is safely gathered in'.

AUGUST

August 24th, St. Bartholomew's Day, night of the cold dew

BEYOND THE LITTLE HAMLET where we live, a cart track runs along beside a field of Barley now awaiting its day of harvesting. The track at this time of the year is a riot of wild flowers and grasses, grasshoppers chirp unseen where Poppies flaunt their scarlet petals among the blue of the Scabious and bright purple Knapweeds, known always to country folk as Hard Heads. The sky blue of the last of the Cranesbill entwine with the white and pink Yarrow, which stands tall and strong, whilst beneath them scramble the yellow, orange-tipped eggs and bacon, the country name for Birdsfoot Trefoil. All these mixed with the deep pink Clover flowers.

Bees of all description are busy collecting the pollen, and the dog disturbs clouds of butterflies making the most of the sunshine to collect their fill of nectar. Among them are the speckled Marble Whites, Meadow Browns, Ringlets, Graylings, Skippers and Tortoiseshells. They hover round the flower heads making a moving halo of blurred colour, and from the flowers and Barley ripening in the sun comes the familiar scent of a late summer's day.

Further along the path a swarm of distressed wasps is busy trying to repair their home, a hole in the bank, which has been dug out by Brock the Badger, searching for honey, his thick pelt making him impervious to the stings of the furious wasps.

This track which I walked along was once the road leading to a farm house, which lies about three miles from the hamlet. A lonely farm amidst the Downland, overlooking the site of what is believed to have been a medieval village. This farm has long been thought to be haunted and has an air of mystery surrounding it.

Not far away, running along the crest of the Downs, is the ancient Ridgeway, where once the Knights Templars rode out to escort and protect the pilgrims as they made their way along the track. Walk along that part of the Ridgeway and there is the feeling that one is never alone, but there is a presence still on guard, and one can almost see, on a slight hill, the shape of a figure mounted on a grey horse, holding aloft the emblem of the Knights Templars, the red cross on a white background.

As I wandered along the footpath by the cornfield on that hot August day, I thought of the people who had trod that path many years ago on their visit to the market town of Marlborough, five miles away. Perhaps they would have been given a lift on some farm wagon, or carrier 's cart, and what a bumpy ride it would have been, as the wheels lurched from side to side in the ruts. I can imagine some little servant girls and ploughboys from the farm saving their meagre wages to spend at the Mop Fair, which is held in the nearby town in the Autumn. By then the track would have become wet and muddy. The way must have seemed so very long, after a tiring day's work on the farm. The night would have been filled with country sounds of sheep bells tinkling from the sheep folded for the night on the Downs nearest the farm. Owls calling from the wood, and the sharp bark of a vixen, as she crept along by a hedge. The thought of the Fair, with its lights and noisy bustle, must have urged on those tired feet.

Now, on the night of the Fair, as I sit by the fire in my cottage by the lane, along which they would have passed, I imagine I can hear footsteps hurrying along to the Fair. I know really it is the sound of the dry Autumn leaves being whirled along by the wind. Or is it?

Where are the roundabouts, barley sugar bright?
  Brassy organ music drifting through the night.
Stripy, sticky sweetmeats, gaudy balls on jerky string,
  Swingboats, and coconuts, and stalls of pretty things.
Country folk a-resting now harvest time is done.
  Pennies in their pockets, out to have their fun,
Just one eve of pleasure a time of chat and joy,
  Where neighbour greets neighbour,
      and surely girl meets boy.

MID / LATE AUGUST

THE ROWAN BERRIES ripen to a glowing orange. Young Blackbirds, aided and abetted by Father, gorge on the berries, whilst at night young Owls call from the Lime Trees.

Heavy rains beat down the Oats still awaiting the combine harvester, and the night sky brilliantly lit with sheet lightning. When, as children, we woke in the night to see from our window the summer lightning, lighting up the fields and woods, we were told not to be afraid, as it was ripening the corn.

Some of the fields are already ploughed, whilst others wait for the sun and wind to dry them out. Then, they too, will soon be stubble ready for the plough.

Many animals in the countryside are on the move, as the harvester disturbs them. Foxes, with cubs now ready to fend for themselves, are taken by the vixen and her mate to visit nearby hen coops, and woebetide any hens that have not been securely fastened in. The fox cubs will soon be shown the quickest way to a chicken dinner!

The Badgers travel abroad by night, unfortunately crossing busy roads, with no thought, or knowledge, of the Green Cross Code, and it is heartbreaking to see those wonderful creatures lying crushed by the roadside.

The Deer, forever nervously on the look out for danger, gracefully dash from cornfields to the shelter of the woodlands. Rabbits and Hares rush from the standing corn to find pastures new, whilst the cock Pheasant shouts loudly to his mate with her brood to 'take care'.

The countryman out and about takes note where the blackberries will soon be ripening. In the woodlands the sweet chestnuts and hazel nuts will be already formed. But whether the countryman, or the squirrels, will get there first is another matter. All these changes are noticed. There is not just corn to be harvested in the countryside in the coming months, but nature's bounty of berries, nuts and mushrooms, together with vegetables in the garden to be gathered and prepared ready to be turned into jams, jellies, pickles and chutneys.

The summer storms bring down the dead boughs and twigs from the trees; these are stored in the barn ready to dry out for kindling, whilst logs are split and stored, the biggest and specially large ones put on one side for the Christmas Yule Log. Under the trees, among the dark green leaves of the ground ivy, the Cuckoopint, or Lords and Ladies, have become a spiral of flame red berries, whilst on a fallen log a riot of amazingly shaped toadstools have turned the dead, damp, wood, into a pattern of beauty.

The cattle and sheep are still happily grazing in grassy meadows, especially in the cool evenings, when the persistently cruel flies have disappeared, and as the moon comes up, known to country folk hereabouts as the 'Parish Lantern', bathing grass and animals with a soft light, the country scene and the bringing in of yet another harvest.

LATE SUMMER

A BEAUTIFUL LATE summer's evening with scents and sounds of harvest in the distance, the day turns hot with a light breeze. Along the narrow lane comes a huge yellow monster of a Combine Harvester, and as I have done for over sixty years I run (to say today I run is a bit of an exaggeration – I hobble fast!) to watch the harvesters go by.

The Combine, with bright orange lights whirling and flashing fore and aft, preceded by a Land Rover flashing warning signals, and with tractors and trailers bringing up the rear. Cars parked outside cottages are hastily driven away before the monster's rumbling approach. The driver of the Combine, sitting aloft in his cabin, just as a captain sails his ship to sea, so the Combine operators sailed their crafts to the waiting seas of ripened corn. As he passed our little white gate, sitting high above me master of all he surveyed, I would wave and wish him well. He nodded and smiled, strong hands steering his charge between the old grey stone walls that border the lane. No doubt he wondered why I stood there. Little did he know I was remembering a time, long ago, when I stood to watch the harvesters turning out from the old farmstead, the great shire horses, the brasses of their harness: glinting and swinging as they threw their great shoulders into their collars to pull the wagons in which stood sun-browned men leaning on their forks, and as they passed on their way to the harvest fields, they laughed and waved their caps. I remembered the days of harvest, with the binder pulled by three or four horses, and how the machinery that tied the sheaves of corn with 'Massey-Harris' twine would continually jam, and with shouts of Whoa there, all would come to a shuddering halt while, with some choice words, the twine would be sorted out, and reaping continued. Should there have been storms of heavy rain and the corn too flat for the binder to reap, men who could use a scythe or hook would reap and tie the sheaves of flattened corn by hand.

Times and machinery have changed, but the men behind the harvesting are still the same breed. Men, whose fathers before them, had to learn new skills to drive and repair tractors and new implements instead of horses and their equipment. Now their sons and grandsons master these great machines that work the land, and I am made aware that those who worked the land long ago have much in common with those who harvest with their great machines. They all were, and are today, masters of their craft. Let us not forget that it is their dedication to get the harvest home, that has remained unaltered through the years.

4 AUTUMN

THE BOWL

In the summer I stand the old blue and white bowl (I suppose it started its life as a soup tureen) in the open fireplace. It is filled with flowers, from the frothy Cow Parsley in May, to the Phlox and gaily coloured Asters, and ears of amber-bearded barley in the early Autumn.

Then, with the nights drawing in and the harvest well on its way, the golden glorious harvest moon hanging above the old cottage, comes the time to light the Beech logs, laid in readiness on the hearth. I wash out the bowl ready to store out of sight at the back of the cupboard, among other less used bits and bobs. As I dried it I looked at its cracked interior. The missing handles, broken off how many years ago? I have never seen its lid. The pattern, a light and dark blue squiggly flower and leaf design, is still bright and clear. The shape of the bowl as lovely, in spite of its cracks, as the day it left the hands that fashioned it.

I remember Mother, many years ago, serving thick delicious soup with dumplings from it. How many delectable mixtures of home-made soups it must have held. Venison, Hare, with vegetables straight from the field or garden, mushrooms, gathered at first light, and aromatic herbs that, as soon as one lifted the lid, would fill the room with that mouth-watering smell.

When it was no longer used for cooking purposes, the bowl was placed in the dairy, and precious lemons stored in it. With a plate of water placed on top, the lemons kept for ages.

When we left the farm the old bowl was put aside and forgotten until I came across it and used it for my cottage flowers. Looking at the old bowl again, I could not bear to store it away, so now it stands proud and glowing, a round satisfied feel about it, on the kitchen dresser, filled with brown eggs, no longer alas, gathered warm from the rickyard (looking up the eggs, as we say in Bedfordshire) as in years gone by. But at least they come from hens free to scratch and feather dust and move freely. The bowl, once again, is doing an all the year round job, and filling the eye with pleasure.

THE COUNTRY BREAKFAST

SEPTEMBER COMES with misty mornings, and early morning Mushrooms can be found on the Downlands, where the night before there was no sign of one, and the time during a mild spell to rise early and gather from the Downlands the Mushrooms, white capped, pearl pink underneath, and smelling the fresh Autumm earthy smell remembered all one's life. When searching, with eyes still a little sleepy, one comes across the fairy ring, some just pushing through the ground and weaving a criss-cross pattern across the top of grasses, others big as small saucers. Then, under the trees that line the meadow, hidden among nettles, grow the Horse Mushrooms darker brown underneath and some as big as dinner plates. What flavour!. As we place them carefully upside down in our basket our mouth waters at the thought of breakfast. The big old frying pan taken down (this pan was never washed or scrubbed, but wiped clean and never known to stick). The fire now well drawn up and glowing red, a little dripping placed in the pan, some thick slices of bacon (once from the home reared killed and cured pig – what a difference in flavour to that we buy today). Some left-over cold potatoes, chopped and fried crisp with the bacon, then placed on the old blue rimmed serving dish and put into the oven to keep warm. Some slices of bread fried crisp and placed with the bacon and potatoes. The brown eggs from the chickens, which wandered at will around the cottages, but not allowed in the garden, with deep golden yolks, cracked into the pan and cooked to individual requests. Some like them with soft yolk, some have them turned over so the yolks are set and the whites have frilly edges. Then the mushrooms, peeled and washed, put into the pan with pepper, salt and a small knob of dripping, fried gently for a few minutes.

The table is laid with a chequered cloth, a pot of butter and a brown crusty loaf. Toast and home-made marmalade, with glowing golden rind in its pot. There is no need to call that breakfast is ready. The smell of the cooking has everyone ready and waiting. The dish is brought laden to the table and, though perhaps we do not clasp our hands in prayer, in our hearts we give thanks that we are able to enjoy such fare. The task of wiping the empty dish clean with a piece of bread to sop up the juices left is much sought after and had to be taken in turns. Much cheating is known to take place to obtain this cherished last morsel. We are then ready to begin our daily tasks

SEPTEMBER

THE COMBINES have been busy and already some fields have had the cultivators through them. The lanes are busy with tractors and trailers loaded piled high with corn. Notices appear on road sides 'Beware tractors turning'. Straw litters the roadside. To older country people the sight of straw lying there can turn the heart, bringing back memories of long ago, of stack yards, busy with men's voices. Horses and carts piled high with sheaves. The ride to the harvest fields in the empty wagons pulled by the great Shire Horses, so big, so kind. They would lower their heads that a child might stroke their velvet noses. The fields where men, in shirt sleeves and waistcoats, pitched with strong sinewy sunburnt arms, sheaves of corn, with a grace and beauty of movement that lasted until dusk. The fields echoed to the shout of the boys leading the horses from shook to shook of corn of 'O, G', which is a shortening of 'Hold Ye'. Woebetide any wagon that moved before the 'O, G' was shouted, as the man loading on top of a cart of slippery sheaves, unless his pitchfork is well prodded into the load to hold him steady, could easily fall.

September is also the gardeners' harvest time. The long hours of Spring and Summer seeding, planting, hoeing and watering, feeding, destroying pests, scaring birds and pigeons from succulent green vegetables, praying and cursing, now show the fruits of that labour. Runner beans hang straight and tender, ready to be picked and prepared for the freezer. The early apples, the little Summer apple, already taken. The Victoria Plums quickly gathered and safely put out of the greedy wasps' way. Onions pulled and left to dry, as are the shallots. The perfect ones put on one side for seed.

OCTOBER

MAIN CROP POTATOES are lifted and safely stored. Greenhouses made ready to receive tender plants at the first sign of frosts, and, as the days shorten, in the cottage fires are lit in the evening for warmth before retiring to bed. Whilst in the larder the shelves are filled with jars of glowing preserves and pickles, the ingredients garnered from the kitchen garden, or hedgerow.

During October the Comice pears (the king of all pears) are gathered from the tree trained along the garden wall. They are carefully placed on paper-lined shelves in the fruit store to finish ripening, ready for the fruit bowl on the sideboard in the dining room, and making a delicious juicy dessert at dinner.

Apples are also gathered and stored safely away, and what lovely names spring to mind, some varieties fading from memory – Peasegood, Nonsuch, Annie Elizabeth, Rev. Wilks, Herrings Pippins, and the better known Ribstone Pippin, Coxes Orange Pippin, Blenheim Orange, Russet and Bramleys.

The nuts are gathered from the stand of Hazels, though it is a race against the squirrels – who watch every movement from their vantage point high above in the nearby beech trees. Conkers, so beloved by school children are removed from their bursting prickly shell cases, and I can never resist their shiny glossiness, to put and carry one in my pocket. I find their smooth roundness helps the movement of arthritic fingers. The full moon this month is often referred to as 'The Nut Moon', and no doubt helped those to find and pick the nuts in the shortening daylight hours.

Most of the Swallows have now collected together and made off for their long journey to Africa, and how sad we are to see them leave. On looking up from digging the flower borders, in which lupins and delphiniums have been planted, we watch, flying high above us flocks of swallows and House Martins, probably, late hatching, making their way towards the coast.

Mid October – early November sees more activity in the farm yards and stables as cattle and horses are brought in from the fields. Straw and hay are carted to stables and byres. In the stables the summer sheets for the horses are exchanged for the thicker winter rugs. The sheep are also brought in from outlying fields to be housed nearer the home farm.

The trees are clothed in their autumn colours, and as November approaches high winds bring the leaves tumbling down lining the ground and paths, which become a crunchy carpet if the weather is crisp and dry, or a soggy carpet if wet. The leaves must be swept from the lawns and added to the compost heap, which lurks behind the laurels and hidden from visitors to the garden.

NOVEMBER

NOVEMBER CAN ALSO BE a dreary month, but, as with all seasons and months it has its beauty when, as so often happens after windy weather, the sunsets have a special wild loveliness. The weather often turns cold, and warm gloves and scarves are the order of the day. And wellington boots, or strong boots a must for gardening, or walking the lanes and downland. There always seems to be a Robin in attendance when digging, and often there is suddenly a day when it becomes warmer (known as a weather breeder) when above the wind a Thrush can be heard singing his whisper song reminding us 'if winter comes, can spring be far behind'.

Meanwhile, all the burnable rubbish from the garden, plus old rubber tyres, paper sacks etc., etc., are heaped on a spare piece of ground well away from the buildings, ready for the Fifth of November Guy Fawkes bonfire night. I remember as children we always used to make our Guys, using a broom handle, covered in old worn out clothes, with a turnip for a head. All day was taken up making this magnificent fellow, and we thought darkness would never come. But at last, the bonfire was lit, and with sparklers held in gloved hands, a few golden rains and a couple of rockets showering down on us golden stars, a handful of jumping jacks to frighten the life out of us. All this was followed by potatoes in their jackets roasted in the bonfire, and we really felt the Fifth of November a great occasion. Nowadays fireworks seem to consist of terrific loud explosions, and to celebrate any occasion. How the poor wild life, and domestic animals must suffer!

Now we burn our rubbish, but eat our jacket potatoes in comfort by the fire indoors, and remembering the bonfire night of long ago, when a box of sparklers was a luxury.

The weather now changes from day to day. Daylight hours are shorter and walking home I noticed the wind-smudged smoke from the cottage chimney, and mouse-grey clouds ceaselessly wandering across a sky of pearl. Some trees, now leafless, stand darkly etched in the late afternoon light. The ploughed fields are almost maroon-colour with streaks of chalky pinkness, where the strong south-westerly wind has dried the surface. A sudden squall of rain causes me to hasten into the cottage, to heap more logs on to the fire to make all warm and cosy for the evening.

As I turn the tap to fill the kettle to boil for tea, I ponder how easily these days we turn on the tap and water gushes out. Not so many years past our grandmothers, especially in country districts, used every drop of water. Lucky the ones with a well in the garden and menfolk at home, or children old enough to haul up the bucket of water.

The farmhouse where I was born had the luxury of two hand pumps, one for soft water (which smelt in the summer months). This was for filling the copper on washdays (always on a Monday), and the other for drinking water. We were brought up to conserve water, and never allowed to wash our hands under a running tap, or let water run away down the sink. In the summer all water used had to be in a bowl, and the water afterwards used to water plants in the garden. Now the water in the cottage comes through pipes to taps from a reservoir high on the Downs, clear clean water, and how we notice the difference in taste when we visit those who have chlorinated water. Our cottage still has its well, which could be used, if needed.

With December drawing near, fruit is prepared for Christmas puddings, mincemeat and cake. One can now buy dried fruit packaged ready washed, but years ago we washed and stoned fine plump raisins, currants and sultanas, and these were spread out on a clean tea towel to dry. Stoning raisins was quite a task. A damp cloth was provided for sticky fingers, and a closed mouth was required. My mother never seemed to weigh her ingredients, but knew if we had succumbed to temptation and ate the fruit! Once the puddings had been made they were steamed for eight hours, then covered with a clean white pudding cloth and stored on the dresser shelf, ready to reheat on Christmas Day. The Christmas Cake was made, placed in the oven and, with much debating as to whether it was cooked, or not, a skewer would be inserted, hoping it would come out clean to show it was ready to be removed from the oven. When cold the cake would be wrapped in greaseproof paper and stored in an airtight tin until the day to remove it from the tin to ice and decorate. (Now where did I put those Christmas Cake decorations?).

Brussels sprouts are picked from the garden; and carrots, which have been stored safely from the frost, together with bright-skinned onions taken from one of the many ropes hanging from the shed roof, are taken to the kitchen.

Holly bushes are looked over for berried branches for decorating the manor house and cottage, and suitable sprigs cut for a wreath for the front door.

When weather permits good rich farmyard manure is dug into the ground ready for spring planting.

To all things must come change, and the Estate, having remained virtually unchanged for the past forty years, has been sold. This small hamlet must have experienced many such changes through its existence, causing the inhabitants of the cottage many anxious moments as to the difference the changes would make to their lives. Many are the changes to the Manor house itself, now standing empty after the family have left for their new home.

The builders, having begun alterations to the house and left for home for the weekend, I wandered one misty November late afternoon across the lawn and peered through the blank windows. Somehow in that misty gloom I felt as if I had stepped back into the past, and I was looking into a room where lamplight gleamed on the silver and glass; where firelight flickers on to the richly carpeted and polished furniture. Through the door I see a figure carrying a tea tray laden with silver teapot and muffin dish. I hear the pattering of paws as the family dogs realise it's time for tea, and have risen sleepily from the fireside. I imagine I hear footsteps approaching along the tiled hall, but I cannot see who is coming, but a swish of skirts, the sound of voices – then the moment passed and I am alone. I turn to walk back to the cottage where lights shine out beyond the windows across the paddock, and, as I turn I tell those ghosts I will keep faith with you whatever changes take place. I shall not forget those who, long long ago lived in the old house. Those who also loved its sense of peace and security, and of the sad and happy times experienced there.

. . . and he felt in his heart their strangeness
their stillness answering his cry,

while his horse moved, cropping the dark turf
  'neath the starred and leafy sky;
For he suddenly smote on the door even
  louder and lifted his head :-
'Tell them I came, and no one answered,
  That I kept my word, he said

(from 'The Listeners' by Walter de la Mare)

As the shortest day draws near, more time is spent in the evenings by the fireside. Thankfully the shed is well stocked with split logs, mostly of Beech, but mixed among them are a few of apple wood, which gives off a lovely scent when they are burning brightly. A large basket standing by the hearth and filled with logs, and each morning the fire is laid with kindling, which has been gathered from beneath the trees after a strong autumn gale (it's an ill wind!). With plenty of books and catalogues of spring bulbs and plants to study and decide on the next year's planting of the garden, the evening passes quickly in the warmth and cosiness of the cottage and we drift into day dreaming.

I wonder what springs to mind when homely things are mentioned in conversation? To each one it must bring a different memory. To me there are so many sights and sounds and feelings that convey the word 'homely'. The kettle gently sighing on the kitchen range. The smell of freshly baked bread and cakes; linen newly ironed. Walking into a room where the furniture has been recently polished with old-fashioned bees wax. The sight of a cat with paws neatly folded, blinking into the fire: whilst the old dog opens one eye and thumps its tail in greeting, as you enter. Silver and copper gleaming in the firelight's glow, whilst in the garden the scent of age-old flowers – deep crimson Peonies, full of summer warmth; sweet-smelling Pinks and Phlox; Foxgloves with their spotted flowers, which invite small fingers to explore within; bright orange Marigolds, so aptly named; smiling pansy faces of deep velvety colours, and so many more flowers known and loved since childhood.

Perhaps most homely of all is light streaming through the cottage windows and, as darkness falls, welcoming all who enter through the little white gate, whose woodwork is worn by the many hands who, down the ages, have pushed it open to walk along the flower bordered path leading to the cottage.

5 WINTER

CHRISTMAS

WE NOW BEGIN to prepare for Christmas. The best of the Chrysanthemum blooms cut for the house and Church. Vegetables gathered together and piled high into baskets ready to be taken into the kitchen, enough to last throughout the festive period.

We bring out the box of tree decorations a few days before Christmas Eve, much to the dog's delight, as she knows there is always a treat put on the tree for her. The same decorations are used each year, the same lopsided angel, for the top of the tree, and the same silver, red, blue and green baubles. As we decorate the tree, a job Peter helps with, (but he is never keen when it comes to dismantling it!).

I remember how my Mother always told us of the sugar pig. She was born on 31 December 1882 and christened Eva Eliza. When she was a few years old her Mother died and she was looked after by an older sister. My Mother was very unhappy and longed for her Mother. One Christmas she was given a penny and allowed to choose a sweetmeat from the little village shop. She chose a sugar pig with white and pink blotches. Happily she ran home to show her sister, who, for some reason, was not pleased and knocked the sugar pig out of her hand and it fell to the floor and broke into fragments. This disaster remained in my Mother's mind all through her life, and many is the time the story was repeated at Christmas to make sure her children knew how lucky they were to have more than one present. My Mother died a long time ago and for many years I put a sugar pig on our tree, but for many Christmases I. have been unable to buy one. No sugar pigs, only sugar mice! Then, a year or so ago one Christmas morning I undid a parcel, which was wrapped in pretty paper and placed under the tree and, to my great joy and surprise, in the parcel, from my great, great niece, Georgia, (my Mother's great, great granddaughter) was a pink and white sugar pig!!

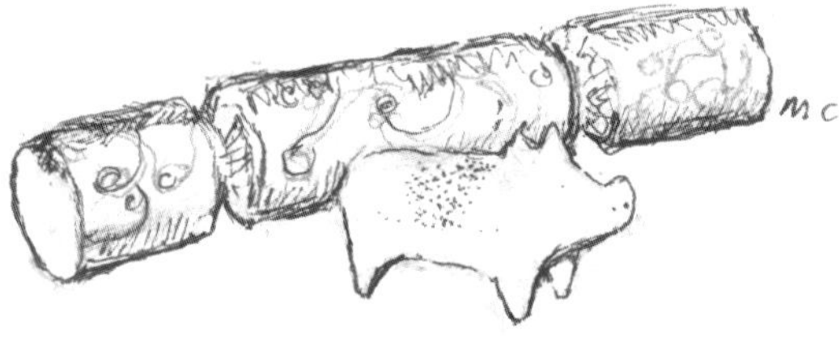

Shortly before Christmas each year Old Jim, who had lived in the village for many years, but latterly had moved into the nearby town, is collected and taken to the little church yard where he places a holly wreath on his baby daughter's grave. Afterwards he visits the cottage for a mince pie and glass of sherry and sitting by the fire tells us stories of his life in the village long ago. Of the sheep (Hampshires) folded on the downs and the music of the sheep bells wafting on the wind over the valley and hills, with its bellwether (the leader of the flock carrying a bell fastened round its woolly neck). Many of the bells had a different note, and the shepherd would recognize each one. 'Lovely it were to hear them,' he said, 'especially when they had they Latten Bells'. I asked him what kind of bells they were and, as is usual for an old countryman, he seemed surprised I did not know. 'Why' he said 'they small round 'uns'. I looked up 'Latten' in the dictionary and found

> *LATTEN: (i) an alloy formally made of, or made to resemble brass, hammered thin, and used in the manufacture of Church vessels; (ii) any thin sheet of metal especially of tin.*

No longer do we hear the sound of sheep bells on the downs, and only once in my life have I heard them. I was walking in another county and from a meadow hidden from me by high hedges, I heard a sound I recognised at once as sheep bells, although I had never heard them before. On peering through the hedge there, sure enough, was a flock of Jacob's sheep, with a fine specimen bearing a bell, fastened round its neck with a wooden frame collar.

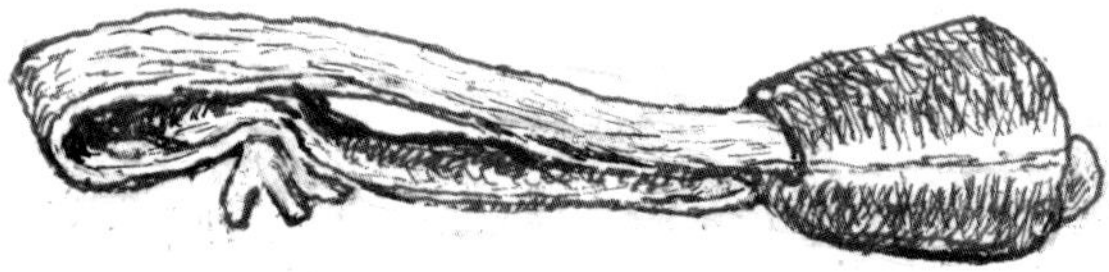

The cottage is decorated with holly and ivy and old-fashioned paper chains. Christmas cards line the window-sill and hang along the beams surrounding us with memories of friends and relations, their loving thoughts filling the room with a kind of glow. All is bustle in the kitchen preparing the Christmas goodies. Presents are secretly wrapped and hidden away ready to be placed under the tree.

Along the lane come the Carol Singers collecting for the parish church. We open the front door and into the cottage floods the sound of the much loved old carols which we join in singing, including 'Away in a Manger' and 'While Shepherds Watch Their Flocks by Night', and when they have finished entertaining us crowd into the cottage for mince-pies, hot from the oven, and mulled wine. How good it is to know that in this small village the tradition of Carol Singers continue visiting each cottage, and long may they do so! 'While Shepherds Watch' seems so right for these Wiltshire downs which still carry their flocks of sheep.

CHRISTMAS DAY

THINKING BACK to when I was a child, waking on Christmas morning, whilst it was still dark, and feeling those exciting packages filling the pillow case which had been placed at the foot of the bed. Thus, having made sure Father Christmas had visited, I called out for a candle. In all probability my poor parents had just drifted off to sleep. Although I was the youngest by far of four children, the others never destroyed my faith that Father Christmas and his reindeer would come, but I admit I did wonder how Uncles and Aunties managed to convey to him which gifts they wanted to give me.

Always on Christmas morning Father would play 'Oh Come All Ye Faithful' on the wind-up gramophone. Even though, living on a farm, animals and poultry had to be fed and made comfortable and the cows milked, Christmas was always a special day. Aunts, uncles and cousins often spending time with us and all gathering round the large kitchen table for a traditional dinner of roast turkey, followed by Christmas pudding and Mother's special trifle. Christmas day was the only day that I can remember Father doing the carving. He stood at the head of the table, knife poised

(Mother probably shut her eyes) and said his Christmas prayer – 'Thank God and Mother for this Christmas dinner. Amen'.

Christmas to many people can be a sad and lonely time, and not everyone celebrates the birth of Christ. But I am so lucky I spend Christmas with those I love, and we carry out the traditional Christmas of old. To me Christmastide should be a time of sparkle (forget the days of never-ending shopping and loud music in the stores and shops bursting with useless, or, too expensive gifts). The short dark and often dreary cold days need shining lights and merriment to get us through this time of the year. A Christmas tree with lights shining in many a window always gives me pleasure, and we always try to leave a light shining in the cottage window on Christmas Eve. I would hate to think there was 'No room at the Inn' here.

The midnight service in the parish church, with lighted candles and the crib so lovingly put together by the children. The carols sung with feeling by the villagers who, for many years, have come to this midnight service. It lifts the heart and conveys the real meaning of Christmas. Of the joy of giving (and receiving also can be a joy), and coming out from the old grey church, wishing all a Happy Christmas. Perhaps some years a flurry of snowflakes greets us, making white the Christmas of many Christmas cards a possibility. Then home to a hot toddy and for me prodding a few of the parcels under the tree, watched by all to make sure I don't 'accidentally on purpose' undo one! The opening of presents takes place in the afternoon after the Queen's speech, when we are all so full of Christmas fare we are almost unable to move.

Then, after a good night's sleep we get ready to prepare the Christmas dinner. The turkey, already stuffed with herbs gathered earlier from the garden and mounds of potatoes, parsnips and Brussels sprouts prepared ready for roasting or boiling. Arguments as to how much does the bird weigh and how long will it take to cook? The Christmas puddings already hubbling and bubbling since early morning. 'Who is going to make the gravy, lay the table with snow-white cloth and sparkling glass and silver?' 'Where are the crackers?' I am sure there are many who remember when celery was covered in soot black clinging soil. No-one wanted the job of washing and cleaning it in cold water! But all enjoyed the crispness and sweetness of that Fen-grown celery.

I still make the trifle, as my Mother made it, and always in the same old dish, which is now pottery-crazed and will not, I fear, see many more Christmases.

The kitchen is filled with delicious cooking smells, a glass or two of wine taken to give us strength to lift and carry the food-laden dishes to the table and, then, it is time for dinner! We say the Christmas prayer of Tiny Tim 'God Bless us every one', and then set about eating with a will. Wine is poured, crackers pulled and, with paper hats slipping down over our ears, we read out those perennial jokes. There are many complaints of 'favouritism' if someone has found a coin in his or her portion of Christmas pudding. Then comes the washing up! When once that is done we can relax and, at last, undo those tantalizing parcels.

Christmas evening is spent sitting around the fire, playing cards – the old favourites 'Nap', 'Bidding whist', or a game of dominoes, and always one or two games of 'Tipit' – a game we always played round the kitchen table, and still play today.

And so to bed. Tired and replete, old friends, old times remembered, not always with sadness, but with thankfulness for those happy memories of Christmas gone by.

On Boxing Day, those who can walk on the Downs, or attend the local Boxing Day Meet, or just sit and enjoy each others company. There is plenty of cold food, so cooking is no problem, so long as someone makes Bubble and Squeak from the cold potatoes and sprouts, and woebetide them if it is not made brown and crisp!

Yes, I am lucky! Christmas for me is a time of sparkle, a time when I step back to my childhood and, though I know there will not be a puppy or a pony present these days (each year, as a child, that was my wish), Father Christmas always comes, bless him! Now I wonder, should I have written my Christmas letter asking for that puppy or pony and sent it up the chimney? It worked, once, long ago!

THE NEW YEAR

After Christmas the weather often changes. Although in November and December there might be frosty days, now the cold weather 'sets in' and the ground becomes frozen making work in the garden difficult. Picking frozen brussels sprouts is not very pleasant, and is a task which cannot be done with gloves on. Water troughs become frozen for days on end, and then one realises just how much farm animals drink, as buckets of water are carried to fields and byre.

On New Year's Eve we hope for a clear frosty night so that, when we leave the cottage at midnight to stand on the lawn, we can hear the Church bells ringing out the old year and ringing in the new. January often brings snow, sleet and rain. Much work is done in the potting shed and greenhouse where compost is prepared for the seed trays, and plant cuttings, struck in the previous autumn, are kept watered and weed-free. Some days there is little daylight and we are thankful for warm socks and scarves. But, how lovely, on clear frosty nights are the stars. We have no street lighting in the village to mar our view of them, and they glitter and sparkle as if scattered over a vast velvet cloth. Even on the darkest days in sheltered spots in a mild spell one can come across a daisy in the lawn, and a gorse bush in bloom.

(When gorse is not in bloom, kissing is out of favour!). As we burn logs in the cottage fireplace there is plenty of wood ash to spread on the vegetable patch. Whatever the weather there is always tidying up to do in the garden. Dead leaves and debris brought down by the winds, and animals and birds to feed. At this time of year the garden to the cottage is alive with birds feeding from the many seed containers I fill each day. Great Tits, Coal Tits, Blue Tits, Nut-hatches, Chaffinches, Green Finches, and the Spotted Woodpecker among them. We hear the Green Woodpecker 'yaffling' from the nearby wood and, towards the end of January, the Spotted Woodpecker 'drums' away in the old Hornbeam in the garden. Above the high wind one sometimes hears the Thrush singing, which lifts one's heart and makes one think of Spring. On other days sleet and snow cover the countryside making the bare trees stand out against the skyline, when you can see the beauty of their shape. We are thankful for the warm cottage, and a good suet pudding to keep out the cold, and we will work off those extra pounds and inches sweeping the paths free of ice and snow. Should the ice be thick enough on the village pond there will be skating for those who can, and sliding for those who can't, with many a bump on one's bottom! In the village where I was born the lake in the Manor Park was open to all the village folk so that they could skate, or slide whilst the ice held. Lanterns were hung along the edge, and the colourful sight of that scene remains with me to this day.

I always think in February one can begin to think of Spring as being 'just around the corner', although there is often much bad weather to come. ('As the days lengthen so the cold strengthens') goes the old saying.

The sheep grazing on the downland above the cottage have their fleeces parted by a strong wind leaving a stripe of silver down the centre of their backs.

Now the springs, which fed the bournes, have risen and the streams run where, a month or so ago, no water was to be seen. It is said high winds will often cause the springs to rise. This is mentioned in the Psalms – 'He bloweth with His wind and the waters flow' (Psalm 147, v. 18). These streams are often called 'Hungerbournes' or 'Woebournes' owing to much wet weather in the early autumn having caused a poor harvest, which meant little food for man or beast through the winter. Some years the water table is very high, then the bournes run deep and flow for several weeks. Sometimes very high winds bring great trees crashing down, bringing with them electricity cables, and then the cottage is plunged into darkness. We then have to revert to candlelight. The old pewter candlestick which stood, when I was a child, on the shelf above the kitchen range in the farmhouse, is now with us in the cottage and with its candle ready and waiting to light our way. An old kettle is placed on the burning logs and when boiling a hot drink is made – also two old stone hot water bottles are filled and placed in the bed to warm the sheets! With candlelight gleaming on copper and brass the cottage steps back a hundred years or so, and we sit comfortably and go back into its past. These village cottages have been home to many families, often large in number and, although they were very basic and humble dwellings, with none of our modern conveniences, those living in them must have been thankful for their shelter and fireside warmth.

CANDLEMASS

FEBRUARY 2ND IS CANDLEMASS DAY. 'The farmer should have by Candlemass Day half his straw and hay'. 'Warm and sunny on Candlemass Day saddle your horse and go buy hay'. These old country sayings tell us quite plainly that, although there are signs that Spring is on its way, Winter is very much with us and snow is still a possibility. Even so, we search sheltered places at the bottom of the hedgerow for the first violet buds, and there are signs of Badgers being on the move. Fresh lavatory pits having been dug. Badgers have very clean habits and keep their setts fresh and clean and on warm sunny days put out their bedding of straw and bracken to air.

In the garden when the ground has thawed, the borders are dug over and rose trees can be planted out. Aconites are a pool of gold under the beech trees, snowdrops and crocus are showing everywhere, the snowdrops shaking their bell-shaped heads in the wind.

At night, as we sit by the fire, we hear the owl's hooting near the cottage, which is said to be a sign of rain. Then comes the cry of a vixen on the prowl and, far off, comes the answering bark of a dog fox. When there is a sharp frost and a full moon, all the countryside is turned to silver,

Over the land freckled with snow half-thawed
The speculating rooks at their nest cawed
And saw from elm tops, delicate as flowers of grass,
What we below could not see, Winter pass.

(Thaw, by Edward Thomas)

Then, in a few days the wind will change to a warmer quarter and there will be in the early mornings a bird song, and by the roadside the first dandelion flowers of gold can be seen. Celandines with their glossy green leaves and enamelled yellow petals star the ditches.

The gardener's year has turned full circle and now, as the days lengthen even more, digging, raking, hoeing and planting begin in real earnest, each day bringing new growth to all things.

As daylight fades I leave the lights burning in the cottage and the curtains undrawn, and wander along the lane with the dog collecting a few sticks for the fire, gathering a little wool left by the sheep on the wire fence (so handy when washed to soothe sore toes). I love to look back at the cottage and see the lights shining a welcome through and beyond the cottage window.

6 AFTERTHOUGHTS

11 AUGUST 1999 ~ THE ECLIPSE

10.35 a.m.

VERY CLOUDY, standing by hunting gate at the top of Scholars Path, there is a slight breeze, I am alone, as Bonnie-dog is now unable to climb the hill, and Peter is watching the eclipse on the television in the Cottage. All is peaceful, and though so cloudy, the sky is lovely. There are pigeons cooing, and in the church meadow young Hereford cattle are all lying down. A pheasant calls from the wood and is answered by one further away.

10.50 a.m.

I have walked to the standing stone circle outside the wood, and the sun has briefly come out from behind the clouds. I risked a quick glance as I have no eye protection. All around is utter peace. The downland stands empty around me.

Where I stand the harvest has been taken and the oat stubble not yet ploughed in. This reminds me of childhood days of running through stubble fields, with the result of very sore ankles from the sharp stubble! As I stand deep in thought, someone runs behind me through the stubble. At first I thought it was a deer, but it was a young man seeking a group of companions. We exchanged greetings and he sped away. The quietness returned unbroken, the quietness of evening falling even though rooks are cawing as they circle over the downland. Where I stand, the stones are almost covered in grass and weeds, with just the tops showing. The stone circle itself is not old, but the stones that form it are Sarsen stones and very, very, old. How many eclipses have passed over them I wondered?

10.55 a.m.

A light breeze has sprung up and rustles the seed heads of the Hogweed and the seeded docks. It has become colder.

11.00 a.m.

The breeze has dropped, , and at 11.05 a.m. the sun once again peeps out from behind the clouds. I take another quick glance and see a thin crescent of sun. The sky becomes darker grey and so still everywhere. From afar, at 11.10 a.m. comes the sound of someone calling or blowing a pipe or horn. A thin echoing sound floating across the downland, and being answered from a distance – probably the group who was being sought by the young man who passed me earlier. There was no sign of anyone I could see on the wide open downs. There is still light, a kind of dimpsy light, as if evening was turning into night. And so unbelievably still. The far away calling continues for a short while.

11.15 a.m.
The sky, a pearly grey – the colour of the pigeon's feather I had picked up. It is almost dark. The calling has stopped, all is quiet and still. No bird calls now. A great peace descends around me as I stand enthralled alone in this most lovely part of Wiltshire.

11.25 a.m.
The sky lightens. A patch of blue appears, and from the wood a pigeon starts to coo. The land once again grows bright, and I turn and take the steep path for home. There is a strong smell of fox along the path. No doubt it was surprised at the shortness of its nightly hunting. But there was no sign of it anywhere.

I arrived home to the cottage, where from the bushes a wren greeted me with her shrill complaining. The cattle in the meadow were grazing, and the blackbirds were searching for worms on the lawn. Back to a normal day, and memories for me of a never to be repeated experience.

THE VILLAGE INN

HOW CHANGED has the village inn, or public house, become? Once the meeting place for country folk, where talk was of land, horses and cattle, Where farmers meet to settle a deal, or try to make one. The inn, or pub floor could have been of wood, bricks, or stone slabs. The furniture consisted of oak settles (or pews); tables, often scuffed and worn. The farm worker, or villager, would come in with his dog, who would creep beneath the settle where he stayed until his master's boot scraped the floor as he rose to make his way home. 'Baccy' smoke filled the air, and the glasses of frothy ale made wet rings on the surface of the tables. Local gossip, the government, taxes and prices, would be argued over in the bar and tap room. Today, few of those who frequent the local pub or inn work on the land. The bar and tap room floors are now carpeted and furnished with tables and armchairs with various chintz covers. The walls resplendent with horse brasses (many of which have never been near a horse!) and the sad sight of an empty bridle and collar, whose wearers those gentle giants (Shire Horses) have left the village many years ago. There is now quite often a sign on the door 'No Dogs Allowed'. And in the corner stands a fruit machine (or one-armed bandit), or a Juke Box, where for a few coins the tune of the day can be selected.

In times past the village folk made their own entertainment. At the end of the harvest, or Christmas, after a few pints of beer, (often called singing beer), the old country songs would be sung, led by a member of the village, who, for a refill of his glass, would gladly start the singing. A piano would most likely be played to help the singing along. There, in the low-ceiling room, with its smoke-coloured walls, the firelight and lamp lights would make shadows in the corners reflecting the light from the raised glasses. Those playing cards, or dominoes, would stop their playing and join in the chorus. After 'last orders', followed by stop tap (closing time), in groups or alone, they would make their way to cottage, or farm, where a light left burning in the window and a kettle singing on the hob awaited them. Should there have been too much drink taken, perhaps the welcome would be less inviting, and harsh words would greet the homecomer.

One such pub in a village in the Chilterns, I well remember, there were stone steps to the front entrance, and a long stone-flagged passage. On the left was the Tap Room with benches and tables, the windows of which overlooked the village street. Nothing much happened in that village without it being noticed from those seated in the tap room – a new bonnet, baby, or horse coming along the street, and 'Ah sees as Mrs . . . 'as 'er new 'at on', or 'that Glad's got her baby out', and 'Old Tom's 'a fetched that new 'oss he went on about'. The merits and faults of those would keep the tap room occupied for some time. On the right of the passage, down several steps, there was a long bench on which stood the barrels of beer. From these barrels the beer was drawn off into the glass or jug. When the barrels were first broached a wooden mallet was used to knock out the bung and a tap was quickly inserted. A wedge would be placed under the back of the barrels to tip them forward, and as the beer became less the wedge was knocked forward. On the top of the barrel was a hole with a wooden peg, which controlled the air. Usually there would be two kinds of beer served from the barrels – Mild and Bitter – which, when the Inn Keeper or pub landlord knew his job, the beer flowed like 'Nectar from the Gods'.

One man, who helped in the pub during the evenings and whose cottage was nearby, would often drink eight pints or more of this brew, and then, on returning to his cottage after closing time, would sit down to his supper which had been prepared for him by his wife and kept warm on the hob – a large bowl of fresh milk, into which she had added a small white loaf broken into small pieces to which a liberal helping of sugar was added, and a knob of butter. His cottage stood among a small group of cottages bundled together and whose gardens ran parallel to one another. The 'privies' (lavatories) to these little cottages were situated out at the back, often down the garden and were of the wooden-seated variety with one or two 'holes' with a bucket under each. There would quite often be a conversation carried on between those working among the vegetables in the garden and the one seated comfortably (or not) in state on his privy with the door propped open. For generations the contents of these buckets were dug deep into the gardens, which then produced vegetables, unbeatable for size and flavour (Did someone mention 'Organic Vegetable Growing'?)

BENJAMIN ~ DONKEY EXTRAORDINARY

ONE IMAGINES A DONKEY to be humble, servile, stubborn, but kind. Not so Benjamin. Stubborn, yes. Humble, definitely no. This is his story.

Benjamin's father's name was George. His mother, Bridget who, when he was born one lovely May morning in 1968 when the woods were full of blue-bells and the call of the cuckoo, took one look at her son and said thank you, but no thank you. He was just a woolly scrap, with a big head and long ears, dark brown body with a mealy-coloured nose muzzle. Every time he tried to drink from his mother she knocked him over. He was very unsteady anyway on those long wobbly legs. After a few hours I could bear it no longer, and holding him in my arms I vowed he would live. I managed to milk his mother, getting enough cholesterol, which was essential for his survival before the milk ran dry, and there was no more sustenance for her son. Luckily I had been in contact with some people in Scotland who had reared an orphaned donkey foal successfully. They kindly sent me a menu with full instructions on how to take care of little donkeys. Firstly, donkey foals cannot take cows milk, so goats milk was recommended. My husband Peter was sent to search the Parish for a goat in milk. He returned goatless. He was then sent to Boots the Chemist for one of the proprietary baby foods, which was the next best thing. Over the next month or so Peter was a regular customer at the chemists for ever larger supplies. He noticed the girl serving him giving him very funny looks, and he later heard she thought he was keeping a harem somewhere deep in the Wiltshire downs! His mutterings about bringing up a baby donkey did not seem to bring any enlightenment to the girl's manner.

Benjamin was fed every two hours from a bottle which he sucked quite happily, during the day, and every four hours during the night for a few weeks until gradually the night feed was stopped. I am hopeless at keeping awake late at night so Peter did the late night shift and I the early morning one. Ben was so small he could be held in one's arms whilst he drank his milk. Then came the worry. Was his little inside working properly? No trace of what went in seemed to come out the other end, so a call was made to the local Vet, who was very understanding and helpful at calming down a rather distraught me. Liquid paraffin was the answer! Then the decision, how much? I can't quite remember the dose, but can well remember crawling round his straw bedding for the result, and the absolute relief at finding it.

Baby donkeys play and skip around their mothers from a few hours old. This enables them to grow strong and control those wobbly knees. As I had taken over the role of Ben's mother, I spent quite a long time skipping around with him. He would follow me on walks, carrying him home when he got tired. I worried quite a lot about his condition. I felt he was not looking quite as robust as he should. Luckily a friend came to stay, who had cared for many babies. She looked at Ben, said he was not getting enough milk, (I had followed all the instructions) and filling a large bottle picked him up and cuddling him close (she is a large cosy person) fed him his extra ration. From that moment on he never looked back. When the time came for him to take food for himself, I showed him how to chew by nipping off the hawthorn and chewing it myself transferring the mulch to his mouth. He was very quick learning. There has never been anything backward about Benjamin!

Ben spent much time in the garden with my Springer Spaniel, Tarn. Both of them came into the cottage to see what I was doing. Ben used to love standing in the kitchen doorway when I was cooking, stamping his little hoofs on the kitchen floor. I think he liked the noise they made. Both Ben and Tarn would curl up before the open fire. Ben was very clean and always went to the corner of the garden to spend his 'penny' before coming into the cottage.

Alas, baby donkeys grow quite big and strong from birth. Ben's long soft ears always turned over at the tips; these began to straighten. The lovely black cross on his back stood out against his dark brown coat. (the cross which baby Jesus is supposed to have traced with his little fingers when carried with his mother Mary on a donkey's back on their journey from Bethlehem). When Ben had to have more grass we put him into a paddock near the cottage. Oh dear! That was not to his liking at all although he could see me and was visited many times during the day. He was always brought back into the garden for a visit and he refused to return to his paddock without a protest.

Some time later a family moved into the village. The little girl loved to ride Ben and as she was as determined as he was they made a good pair. They spent many hours together, mostly arguing as to whether or not he would go the direction she wanted. When not being ridden he stayed in their garden, and during the time they watched the T.V. they would open the window so that he could also watch. One day he walked into the downstairs bathroom and sampled the soap, which he definitely did not like and showed his displeasure, as was his wont, with his heels sharply rapping the door. Unfortunately the family left, and other children were afraid of Ben's uncertain moods. He was now a strong young donkey with a mind of his own (rather too handy with his hoofs) and very good at making nasty faces at those he thought he could frighten.

My idea of him doing his bit for Charity for those poor donkeys less fortunate than himself, those overworked little donkeys whose patience and suffering we read about and tears one's heart strings, was not his role in life! Although he loved to be near children, I never dared trust him not to kick, as that was his first reaction when frightened, or even annoyed.

So the time came for Ben to be moved to the racing stables in the next village to 'look after' the racehorses. Donkeys are very useful for this, as they do not gallop around and act as pacifiers to the highly-strung thoroughbreds, which are turned out for a rest. Getting Ben to the racing stables was a pantomime, as getting him to go anywhere was a nightmare in itself if he did not feel inclined to go. A horse box was sent for him and no amount of coaxing would get him to enter. Eventually, several strong stable lads arrived and lifted him bodily into the box. He was not amused! At the stables he was well cared for. A friend of ours lived in a cottage at the bottom of his paddock, and made sure all went well with him. The head lad also took care of him and the owners also had a soft spot for him, in spite of his braying outside their window if he thought they were ignoring him.

Among those who visited Ben in his paddock at the racing stables were two young children who lived nearby. They would spend ages sitting on straw bales talking to him, and late one evening Ben decided to visit them. Delicious smells were coming from the kitchen. Their mother being a wonderful cook, Ben thought he would investigate and finding a weak spot in the fence he arrived at the kitchen door to the surprise and delight of the children. Alas, Ben refused to return to his paddock. No way could he be moved, so the owner of the racing stables was sent for. Unfortunately he had decided on an early night after a busy and tiring day, and clad in pyjamas and dressing gown and not, as one can imagine, best pleased, he attempted, with the help of his dressing gown belt, to remove Ben. Watched by the family and a few onlookers, Ben suddenly threw up his heels and with head down charged through the trees while a very irate racehorse trainer attached by his dressing gown belt was pulled back to his paddock.

Among the many racehorses he 'helped train' were Bishops Bow; Run Hard; Successor; April the Seventh (who won the Whitbread and the Hennessy). When the owner of the racing stables died, his son carried on at another racing stables. Ben went with him and there 'helped train' the Grand National winner Maori Venture.

Owing to the lack of grazing Ben came home to me at Rockley and lived in a paddock with a shelter at the bottom of the cottage garden. He would stand in his shelter when the weather was fine but, being Ben, stood out in the rain. The highlight of his life was a bonfire. As soon as one was lit he rushed up to put his great head over the fence to be as near to the smoke as possible. His ears went back and he positively leered as he stamped his hoofs in anger, or pleasure, I never could decide which. At any rate a smoky bonfire 'sent him'.

His hooves were regularly attended to by our friend Terry, who had held him in his arms when a tiny foal. But, however, having his feet made smart and comfortable was not one of his pleasures, and he showed his disapproval in every way possible.

During the winter months he decided no donkey worth his salt would deign to graze on common grass, so at the first sign of a light being switched on in the cottage in the morning, he would give a great shout and one of us would stagger out (often me in wellington boots and night-gown and dressing gown) to feed him his breakfast of hay and a mixture of nuts bran (and, don't tell anyone, a few oats) for his pleasure. During the day, if it was cold and frosty, a call for sustenance would shatter the peace of the village, and if we went out in the car he had a vantage point where he could see our return. I swear his counted the number of carrots I was staggering along the path with and if not enough would demand more! At Christmas he had his stocking, as did the dog. Ben's treats were chocolate biscuits. On Christmas Eve we would creep to his shed just to see if he was kneeling. Although he was no Ox:

> Christmas Eve, and twelve of the clock.
> 'Now they are all on their knees',
> An elder said as we sat in a flock
> By the embers in hearthside ease.
>
> We pictured the meek mild creatures where
> They dwelt in their strawy pen.
> Nor did it occur to one of us there
> To doubt they were kneeling then.

(Thomas Hardy – The Oxen)

On Palm Sunday he was given a special treat of polo mints and carrots and was made clean and tidy, just in case he was needed!

> . . . Fools! For I also had my hour;
> One far fierce hour and sweet;

There was a shout about my ears,
And palms before my feet.

(G.K. Chesterton – The Donkey)

At Eastertime he had his hot cross bun and Easter egg. He looked on all this as his rightful due and gave no thought to his brethren elsewhere in the country or world plodding sandy beaches or carrying heavy loads, etc.

Alas, once again we had to find him fresh pastures and were lucky enough to find a very kind couple who lived in an old mill house who needed a companion for their donkey Rascal. So Ben, reluctant as ever to get into transport, was carried in style to his new paddock, which had a very comfortable shed. Two doors so each donkey had its own entrance. Here he was treated as royalty having home baked brown bread made from organic flour and, at Christmas, each donkey had its own Christmas pudding, hand made specially. We could visit him whenever we liked and sometimes he seemed pleased to see us, other times, Ben like, his attitude was 'go away, I don't wish to be bothered'. Ben lived with them for several years, and then friend Rascal died. Some time after he got stuck in the mire, a boggy patch at the old millrace (where he had no business to be). Vets were called, all the family rushed to help one very sorry donkey. However all was well and Ben soon recovered, but developed what we all thought was arthritis. Some mornings he could not stand on his feet after lying down.

He was a heavy chap and impossible to lift, so it was decided he should go to the Donkey Sanctuary in Devon, where there are Vets on call. Arrangements were made. I said goodbye to him and pleaded with him to be good. His look in reply to that said he would decide how to behave! But for once he allowed me to stroke those long soft ears with still the little bend at their tips. Just one stroke and that's enough he said. My husband Peter and friend Terry went to help load Ben into the horse box for his journey to Devon. I was told such a kind man came with a collar on which was Ben's name. Phone calls were made to tell of his safe arrival at the Sanctuary. He was visited by kind friends after a few weeks and all were delighted with his care and surroundings. We were to be taken in the Spring to see him and perhaps spend a few days staying near to him. Alas, it was not to be. Ben became ill and after a few months had to be put down. A post mortem showed he had incurable liver disease. We would so much have loved him to have spent at least one Spring and Summer with other donkey friends, in surely what must be a donkey paradise.

We still miss him. Difficult he might have been, but we loved him. Sometimes in the early morning, when the mists fill the hollows of the paddock where Ben once lived, I imagine I see those long ears and hear the beginning of a long drawn out 'He Haw', and then I remember Ben is no longer here, but is very much with us all in our memories.

AFTERTHOUGHTS